THE RESURRECTION OF
STAR
REBELL

Ms. Star Rebell

S.H.E. PUBLISHING, LLC

The Resurrection of Star Rebell

Copyright © 2024 by Ms. Star Rebell

For information contact:
info@shepublishingllc.com
or visit www.shepublishingllc.com

Library of Congress Control Number: 2024945750

ISBN: 978-1-964061-13-9 (paperback)

First Edition: October 2024

10 9 8 7 6 5 4 3 2 1

This book is dedicated to those who recognize life's journey is not a subdued walk into the night, but a journey of personal growth paved with misunderstandings, criticism, and sacrifice. If you are one of the fortunate, amid life's journey, you can be reborn.

A Letter to You

A Letter to You From Me, Star Rebell

Tears rolled down my face while my pen and paper danced in undeniable truth. I paused to laugh, scream, and even sit in awe, reminiscing about the mountains I could hardly climb. "The Resurrection of Star Rebell" is my journey of redemption. Please keep in mind that I do not share my journey haphazardly, but rather to inspire, uplift, and encourage you. My story is not endowed with sparkles, glitter, or yellow brick roads. On the contrary, it is often gut-wrenching and defies the logic of sanity. Somehow, in the end, it became medicine for my soul.

As much as I wanted to stay above water and float on the subtle waves of life experiences, I knew it would rob me of the opportunity to share unfiltered truths saturated with honesty. So, I pulled off my life jacket and dove deep into the swampy grave where all my lies and denials lay. Even when the murky waters made breathing difficult, I bathed in unflattering honesty.

My journey has foul language, sexual content, adult situations, and remnants of life's most complicated challenges and heartache. It necessitates courage for you to take this journey with me. It takes an open mind, personal reflection, emotions you have buried, and possibly emotions you never knew you had.

For that, I say thank you.

A Letter to You

A Letter to You From My Sister

Where should I begin? How do I detail the only individual, other than my parents, whom I have known for all my life? It is like opening a box of a 1,000-piece puzzle and contemplating how to recreate the picture on the box. I think this could be said of Star Rebell and the contents of this book, "The Resurrection of Star Rebell." I will start by connecting the puzzle's corners to Star Rebell.

As you may have surmised, Star and I are sisters. We had the same parents, slept in the same bed, fought over shared clothes, and shed tears of mutual regret. Looking back on my childhood, I idolized my sister. Star possessed all three Ps: pretty, polished & popular. I was so glad when she got braces to close the gap in her teeth, because I then had something I could tease her about, which I did with reckless abandon. To my utter dismay, girls with braces were even more popular than those without! So, for my childhood, I lived in the shadow of my big sister. Although shadows are typically considered cold, dark, and meaningless, I learned not only to love Star but also to appreciate our differences and embrace our uniqueness. Through the years, I have witnessed Star's many successes and failures. I have watched her rise out of the ashes of despair and extreme trauma with the tenacity of a pinned bull released to go after the rodeo clown.

If "fake it 'til you make it" was a person, it would be Star. After reading the book, you'll understand why I say this. For the majority of her life, she suffered through significant losses quietly.

She showed up day after day, month after month, and played her part. When I hear people say, "Fake it 'til you make it," I cringe in disagreement but understand that sometimes it is a necessary strategy for survival. It is so easy to lose yourself in grief, self-pity, and a roller coaster of emotions to the point of no return or extreme despair. This type of despair leads you to put the cover over your head, turn your phone off, close the blinds in your home, and lock the world out until you have rendered yourself unreachable. I have experienced that dark place in my life several times, until I grew in faith and maturity to know that isolation is the greatest apparatus of self-destruction. In silence, your thoughts of despair reign supreme, without any opposition to face.

In "Resurrection of Star Rebell," the familiarity of those silent, deafening valley experiences Star encountered and eventually triumphed over brought a visceral emotional response. I wept. How was it possible to have an intimate relationship with someone who was still a stranger to you? How often do we only solicit surface encounters with our family and friends for fear of the uncomfortable, often ugliness of one's reality? The sad part is we also miss out on the beauty of true intimacy. This book reminded me of the rewards we reap when we put in the work for self-care and self-betterment, as well as the return we receive from investing in others.

The "Resurrection of Star Rebell" is not just another memoir but a tool to strengthen your will to get out of bed, open the curtains, go for a walk, and, more importantly, have an open and honest dialogue with your friends and family. It is a guide to revealing *the real you to someone you cherish and trust. Star and I have always agreed to make sure ONE person knows what is going on. Whether you choose a family member, a close friend, or your mate, I admonish you to find one person with whom you can be completely honest. We all have watched those true crime shows where no one knew the truth about their family/friend/colleague who was suffering some terrible misfortune. Do not be that person!*

Regardless of how ugly you think your truth is, someone has experienced the same thing or something similar. As you turn the pages of this book, I hope you come out of the shadows, cultivate self-love, and identify someone who will walk through life's hills and valleys with you. Remember, self-love and support are essential for personal growth.

Here's to the resurrection of you!

THE RESURRECTION OF
STAR
REBELL

DISCLAIMER

"The Resurrection of Star Rebell" is intended for mature readers who value authenticity and are not easily offended by strong language or sexual content. This manuscript has unfiltered adult themes.

Resources are available at the end of the book if you or someone you know is struggling with life's challenges.

Ms. Star Rebell

My Journey

Introduction

She celebrated life by dancing to all the exhilarating beats life moments had to offer. Life was good; it was better than good. Friends loved her, men adored her, and nothing stood in her way. Not even bills prevented her from dancing into an enjoyable time's revolving door. She tossed those bills in the wind like she did the curls in her hair. Year after year, her mantra was trips abroad and flights between paychecks. She was young with nine lives and unaware that even affordable good times would eventually become too expensive.

But for now, she continued indulging in everything the world was selling, regardless of the guarantee. Quick fixes, temporary utopia, and adulterated happiness were all worth the price for a moment of delight. One day, while sitting back, sipping on memories, and listening to old gospel hymns, she was transported back to her childhood church, hearing her dad preach. She smiled momentarily, always proud of his integrity, wisdom, and unwavering character.

Thinking of him always brought her one step closer to running to the altar and cashing in on all her sins for a fresh soul. But her struggles with heartache and secret addictions kept her from recreating the heartfelt scene like the one she saw in The Color Purple. A higher belief saved her dad, but she always struggled with blind faith in something she had so many unanswered questions about, not realizing that one day faith would be the only thing that could save her. I know that because I am her, Star Rebell.

The "Resurrection of Star Rebell" shares my life journey of dancing on broken glass, watching myself get cut, wondering why I am bleeding, and asking for a bandage to heal. After depletion from the regret of addiction, despair from disloyalty, and hopelessness from inner turmoil, life cultivated and inspired me with resilience and love. As you share my journey, I invite you to embrace the tears, laugh aloud, and feel the pain. It is a journey I unapologetically share with you, someone you know, someone you love, and even someone you may become. When you reach life's mountaintop, I hope you will discover renewed determination, grace, and an overflow of self-love.

Life pulled her heart right out of her chest
And called it real love the whole time
Boldly feasting on all of her fears
Like a cannibal devouring its prime
Seeking mercy but no haven insight
She was battered from the turbulent rain
But when she reached life's mountaintop
She could finally appreciate life's pain

Chapter One

Breaking Ground

I was a skinny thing with no shape and a nickname of one of the worst pesty animals alive, a mosquito. With no makeup and a love for ponytails, I was far from winning the award for the cutest girl on the block. But unbeknownst to me, good trouble was right around the corner. I almost lost my mind when my chest started looking like two balloons blessed with helium, and my butt reciprocated the view! Immediately, my self-esteem and cute girl meter went up. It was time to send my mosquito persona on a blind date with a can of Raid. Baby, baby, baby, I was ready for the world!

But do not be deceived. In between flossing and twisting, I made time for church. No matter how hard I tried to rid my system of Sunday service, it was in my blood. Even if I had to go to church in the clothes I just had on the night before, I did.

Nothing else would do when my soul needed to be close to the altar. I blame my parents for that, because they had an unquenchable thirst for a place of worship. Because I was required to attend church so much, I am sure I was born during Wednesday night bible band. At least, that is how I felt growing up as a preacher's kid (PK). I used to tell my folks that we went to church more than Jesus; he was the world's Savior! My goodness, there was a church service for a church service and even one in between. I vowed never to go to church again when I got older. I am sure I did my time, and I had a guaranteed lifetime VIP Heaven membership as a PK.

If you have never been a PK, then you probably know someone who has and hopefully you kept them on the church prayer list! Being a PK made me an easy target for bullies. If I were not cool, it would have been because I was a PK. If I tried to be cool, people quickly reminded me that I could not because I was a PK. My formative years were a struggle. It never made sense why people acted like I was not a regular kid trying to forge my way.

For every mistake I made and even for the mistakes people assumed I made, they all screamed, "CRUCIFY HER." I think Barabbas, a notorious life criminal, got better treatment than I did. The irony is that I had the same struggles as everyone else. My dad decided to spread the gospel, the only difference.

One day, a friend of mine told me about this lady named Karma. I could not believe his words. I was so interested until I begged him, "Tell me more." He continued, "Don't worry about people mistreating you because people always get back what they put into the universe. If they mistreat others, then terrible things will happen to them. That is what Karma does. She always settles the score with people. They cannot escape it." My eyes got so big with excitement and anticipation. I was ready to grab my popcorn and wait for Karma to show up and act a fool on some of these folks! I remember thinking, "Karma is taking her sweet time getting some of these cockroach humans! I do not know if she took a detour, is on a long lunch, or what, but some folks around here still need to be taught a lesson!"

It wasn't until later in life that I discovered that some of those bullies didn't even know what or why they did what they did. The truth is, they, too, had demons they were battling. They were trying to survive and find their way. Just like me. Isn't that strange? I spent all those years envious of people because they were popular or seemed happy when they felt as lonely as me. For some reason, I always assumed people had an extraordinary life if they looked happy. But no one knows what some smiles, laughter, and seemingly perfect lives masquerade.

I remember dating a guy who lived on the thirtieth floor of a downtown high-rise. The first time I went there, the lady behind the desk greeted him with his government name and "MR." in the front. I was shocked at the formality as my mind screamed, "SHUT THE HELL UP!" The lobby had ginormous arrangements of fresh flowers, and when he used his fingerprint to access the elevator, it greeted him with a "Hello." All his clothes were designer, and he only wore Prada and Gucci shoes. And trust me, he wore those labels well! He could be arrogant at times, but not in an annoying way. That is a lie. It just helped that he was charming, and money was never an object.

I remember once asking him why he changed cars so much. He said driving a Porsche was fun for a while but got boring, so he bought a Maserati, and when that got boring, he bought something else. I said, "Okay, that's cool. But why do you get bored?" He said, "Because I am not happy. When I go home, I go home to things, not to anyone or any purpose. So, I get bored easily. Unlike you, you always seem happy, and I wish I could be like that." I looked at him crazy and asked, "Are you sure? I drive a modest car and live in an apartment complex with the same parking lot as Walmart." He said, "Yes, but you are happy." I suppose. I always thought if anybody was happy, it was folks with money. How could they not be happy? It would be incredible to drive the finest cars, have money growing on trees, and live in a building with a concierge. One day, during a heartfelt conversation, I found out he struggled with depression. I was so sad for him. It was so unfortunate. He could afford to buy whatever he wanted, but the one thing he desired most, money could not buy.

Life is peculiar sometimes. I, too, mastered the art of deception so well that it became an ingrained part of my DNA. I forgot how to share, be open, express myself, and even acknowledge my struggles. My mind had convinced me that the only part of me worth sharing with others was the cheerful, carefree side. I had yet to learn how I ended up on that path. Even more so, why did all the signs read DEAD END?

Have you ever looked back on life
Wondering how you got this far
Wondering how you got to this place
No longer knowing where you are

Have you ever thought all was good
Not realizing it was slipping away
Not realizing your silver lining
Was starting to show some decay

Have you ever tried to go back
Searching for what was behind
Searching for a better version
But moments don't have rewind

Have you ever had to start over
Finding your way in the unknown
Finding your way amid uncertainty
On a road, you must travel alone

Chapter Two

Silent Screams

For years, I would not allow myself to feel anything. Whenever I got harsh, unsolicited feedback from those around me, it seemed safer to pretend it was positive. I used to tell myself that maybe they were struggling to deal with their pain, and this was their way to release. Regardless, it did something to me—to my soul. I even went as far as to agree with some of the nonsense to avoid making them uncomfortable or feel bad. I accepted the ridicule and tried to be the person that they, society, and others wanted me to be.

I lost the energy to fight. So, instead, I walked humbly into the sanctuary of denial and self-destruction. The more I internalized things, the worse I got, and the more self-harm I committed. Strangely, people around me did not see it as a cry for help. They only saw it as an opportunity to say that I was a sinner and a wayward child destined for hell.

Preacher: "Wow. Your tattoo scared me."

Me: "Oh...really?"

Preacher: *"Yes, the skull tattoo scared me. I did not know you had tattoos."*

Me: *"Yeah, I've been having them for a long time."*

Preacher: *"Wow...that's scary."*

I did indeed have a skull tattoo on my arm. But on the other arm, I had birds flying, an Ankh (African cross symbolizing life), and a phoenix rising. But of course, the only thing he "saw" and commented about in front of his comrades was my skull. Suddenly, other people were looking at me in shock and disdain. I wondered why he did not take a moment to ask me what the tattoo represented. If he had, he would have known that the tattoos on my right arm, the skull with a beautiful flower trying to grow, stood for a very dark time in my life when hope evaded me, and I almost gave in to the temptress of death.

He would have known that it also symbolized the death of my son, Justin, and my struggle to find joy after his demise. He would have known that the other arm represented my redemption. The Ankh for life, the phoenix rising from ashes, and the word freedom with birds flying free. Every time I looked in the mirror, I knew that there was something beautiful after the pain and heartache. I was encouraged to hold on longer. Around the corner, there was deliverance and healing from agony. However, he never learned that about me. Instead, he knew only that I was the woman with the skull tattoo. Not surprising, though; he was one of many elevated appointees with an opinion. I have been informed....

- The tattoo is demonic
- Your body is a temple
- You have sinned against God
- The devil is using you
- The skull is a symbol of Satan

The list goes on and on. I wanted to invite the "must-call-you-out" crew to sip a strong cup of shut-up! "Seriously, shut up! Sir and Mam, if a tattoo garners so much attention and fear, then you are certainly not prepared to deal with the demonic spirits of the world." That is what I wanted to say to every single one of them. Of course, if I had, I would have gotten holy water shoved down my throat and burned at the altar. Instead, I just smiled.

I was told I wasn't normal
And that I should ask for grace
Being a lady means dignity
And tattoos have no place

I'm sure she's a devil's seed
And indeed she needs our help
Like the woman at the well
She's the reason Jesus wept

But we of course have the answer
How this sinner can sin no more
Cast this demon back to hell
In hell's fire let him roar

Her soul can still be redeemed
Even though she went astray
Now join me my wayward soul
For repentance we shall pray

One day, I pondered. What contributed to me feeling lonely in a room full of smiling faces? It was my willingness to accept whatever someone threw at me. It was my complacency not to speak up even when shit felt like daggers to the heart. I put on the Oscar-winning Strength and No Worries performance until "You can handle it" or "I'm sure it's not as bad as you say" became the status quo. So, I dealt with it. But trust me, my lies could not be buried forever. All the bullshit I allowed was ticking inside of me like a bomb ready to explode.

The most complex life is one that is cloaked in laughter and smiles but meanwhile dying inside. It is like being a fish in water with no ability to breathe. You have gills and a moving mouth, but the air eludes you, and death consumes your existence. I know that feeling. I felt it so much until I started seeing a psychologist. It was the best thing I ever did for myself. I gathered my little inner strength and forced myself to get help. But even that came with ridicule. People who I thought would have been thrilled that I was getting help shunned me. They said I did not need a psychologist; I only needed to read my bible and attend church. But I needed more. That was one time in my life I was grateful I said, "Fuck everybody." If I had not, I would not be alive today.

> *I'm starting a new chapter*
> *Hell no it's a new book*
> *I don't know all the pages*
> *Or how the end will look*
>
> *But I know I will be there*
> *Taking bullshit with stride*
> *Treading friendless waters*
> *Swimming against the tide*
>
> *In secret, I struggled to cope*
> *Depressed, no one knew*
> *Trying to be strong for others*
> *While my marriage broke in two*
>
> *We lost our son at birth (exhale)*
> *He was born into my hands*
> *As our blood engulfed the toilet*
> *I was trying to understand*
>
> *What the hell did I do wrong*
> *That his life wasn't meant to be*

Told in three days I would die
Shit that's fine with me

For years I attempted to love
The person who I was inside
The person who I longed to be
The person they wanted to hide

I can barely trust this moment
I am actually smiling again
After dancing with a gun
Planning for my life to end

After all the shit I endured
I realize this one thing
Life is beautiful and it sucks
But that's not all it brings

Peace and inner strength
Mercy coupled with grace
Dew drops of hope falling
Self-assurance: finding a place

I love you, black Butterfly
And all your nicknames too
I believe in the woman you are
I believe in what you can do

Fly like an eagle daily
Forever spreading your wings
Forever your saving grace
Self-love is a remarkable thing

Chapter Three

I DO

I sleep with you in my dreams
Humming to your soul's lullaby
I lay with you on clouds drifting
As stars dance in the galaxy sky

What I feel is a magical spell
Powerful when it is times two
Beautiful when touched by God
Only right if it includes you

Your voice soothes my mind
Your laughter soothes my soul
Your patience redefines strength
Your presence redefines whole

Desiring for this moment in time
My yesterdays are now made clear
Growth was a required necessity
For Fate to bring us here

I love you forever and always
I welcome that our love is real
Together, our love has a place
That is eternally safe and still

I love you
I always will

I said yes to a man I met on a blind date. Neither of us asked much about the other because neither wanted to go out that night. To our surprise, our date lasted twenty-four hours. He was about 6'3", muscular like Hercules, and had a country accent heavier than ten sacks of potatoes. He was an unexpected Southern gentleman. The fact that he was F.I.N.E. certainly made up for his love of flannel shirts and blue jeans. I, of course, was 5'6" with curves in the right place and a smile that serenaded the moonlight. I had just bought a twenty-six-inch human hair ponytail, so I knew I was a prize. Then, I wore a conservative "I AM CUTE & I KNOW IT' skirt that sparkled with my brown eyes. Trust me; I was the cup of HELLO he did not know he needed. Three months later, he said he loved me, and soon after, we were engaged. Four months later, we were married. It was a fun and exciting time. Everything was perfect.

I had no fears when you pulled me close
Just wondered what took you so long
This moment was worth more than the wait
Inhibitions had no place to roam

Your smile told a gentle story
Of a man with no games to play
Your eyes enjoyed what you saw
While your touch asked me to stay

Everything in life seemed perfect
My heartbeat even took a dance
So much to absorb at once
But I am glad I took the chance

Whatever comes, let it be
With you no fear in my mind
I proudly say forever I DO
As our forevers intertwine

I am not about to deny the fact that we made a gorgeous couple. Life was good. No, life was excellent. No, life was audaciously perfect. I would get up every morning to ensure he had what he needed for work, and then dinner was on the table by the time he got home. I enjoyed being there for him and keeping things going while he was doing the 9 to 5 thing. I spent most of my days watching cooking shows to plan our next meal, with some cleaning here and there. I remember we always had to keep the trashcans empty in every room. I think it was due to his being in the service or something. He said trash in trashcans made the room look unkempt. I was okay with that, considering I had a little "big" touch of OCD, obsessive-compulsive disorder. I was happy.

Nevertheless, during our first year of marriage, there was some adjusting. Why was it so hard to convince him that clothes needed to be removed from the dryer as soon as they stopped to avoid wrinkles? But soon, that became trivial. I was more focused on the spider, which looked like a penny, until I tried to kill it, and suddenly, it became the size of three-half dollars! Literally! What kind of anaconda country bigfoot spider was that?

Not to mention, I had to drive fifty-five minutes to get to Walmart, the only discount retail store around. I'm still clutching my pearls at how people dressed up to go to that place. Some people looked finer in Walmart than in their caskets at the funeral parlor. I am unsure what happened, but somehow, I joined the Walmart Fashion Lukewarm Cult Movement and started doing the same thing. I laid all my baby hair perfectly every time I drove to town. Eventually, I did not even mind the drive because I knew I would see an unbelievable fashion show once I arrived. All I had to do was avoid the chickens, deer, and human-sized possums crossing the road along with horses pretending to be cars. For me to live that kind of life without complaining it had to be love or love's first cousin!

We did not even argue during our first year together. Wait, there was one time when my husband said I was acting like a bitch. Ha. I almost forgot that. I packed up some of my things and told my mom I was coming home and getting divorced. It was over! My mom was shocked, and when I told her what happened, she was like, "Well, is it true?" I was like, "Is what true?" "Is what he said true?" I was like, "Yeah, it is true." Then we laughed so hard that the tears that had dried up on my face came alive again. After talking with her, I had to sit at the gas station for a long minute, trying to save face and eat an entire piece of humble pie. That shit did not taste good, and it took some time to digest. But when I got home, he apologized and hugged me, and it was like nothing had ever happened. We were good at that. We could forgive quickly and get back to loving.

Love is unshaken faith
Believing in the unseen
Trusting in the unknown
Peace in the in-between

Love is a silent hope
Strong when you are weak
Holding on a little longer
Finding what you seek

Love is generously patient
Restoring what was lost
Assurance that it is okay
Worth more than what it cost

Love is you and me
A mystery so divine
Releasing all our doubts
Surviving rain or shine

Love is committed trust
No need to be afraid
Relishing every second
Fruition of what I prayed

Love is echoing, "I DO"
Every time I say your name
Monday through Sunday again
Forever, our love shall reign

We had promises on our refrigerator for a healthy and meaningful relationship. One of the promises was that we didn't have to agree completely to be okay. We could disagree and, five minutes later, share a beer on the front porch. We came into this marriage with two different ideologies, and there were parts of our individuality that would always remain. Another commitment was not to use foul language when upset or in a heated discussion. In the first year of marriage, I broke that one more than he did. However, the one rule we both were passionate about was accepting apologies and moving on. It sounded straightforward, but sometimes simple ain't easy. Lucky for us, it came second nature. My life with him was gracious, exciting, and serene.

We had one corner store in town that closed at sundown. The fanciest eating place was McDonald's, unless you counted the spot with three tables whose specialty was pig feet. I'm sure that was considered fancy eating by some. Country life was a vast difference from the city life I came from. So many of my friends knew I would never trade in my 4-inch heels and silk blouses for rain boots and overalls. But something about the green grass that surrounded our home, the fresh air I can smell even today, and the big oak tree that provided shade year-round, made me complete. I was satisfied.

What is this four-letter word that makes me bold
I want to run to its well, for it quenches my soul

Makes me whole
It is love

What is this four-letter word that makes me cry
I want to conquer my fears and no longer be afraid to try
Makes me high
It is love

What is this four-letter word that makes me hush
I want to surrender my worries and, in it, put my trust
Makes me blush
It is love, your love

The best part about marriage was that my husband allowed me to be me. I remember a couple's date with one of my best friends. We got on stage and danced our hearts out like we were eighteen! The guys were playing pool nearby and kept an eye on us, reliving our youth! We rotated to the bar, often flirting with the bartender, and of course, all drinks were on the house. The guys only wanted to know that we were okay. That was one of the best nights of my life. Well, until my best friend and I started counting butterflies in the venue that did not exist.

My husband never criticized me for enjoying life my way. He encouraged me to grow and evaluate my thinking, but he never diluted my individuality. For the first time, I thought someone could love me for who I was and who I was not. I remember one day asking him why he loved me so much. He said, "Because I don't see you as you are but as you could be." That moment changed my life. Knowing my imperfections, I had never had anyone say no shit like that. Yet he did. That one statement made me want to be the absolute best version of myself, and I believed that the best of me was yet to come.

Years passed, and finally, oh my goodness, guess what? We were pregnant! Yes, to the Y.E.S., we were pregnant! Those were some of the best months of my life. My husband was excited to find out he would be a dad and that we would have a son. I cannot tell you how much we spent to share our love with our newborn baby. We picked out so much stuff and had a list of baby names that was a country mile long. Whenever I looked into my husband's eyes, he was beaming with joy and reading books on how to be the perfect parent. Since I was high-risk, there was little that I could do besides stay in bed and be around the house. But I did not complain once. All the morning sickness, canceling plans because I was nauseous, and craving pickles with peppermint were all worth the feeling of our baby boy growing inside me. There was even more joy when we passed the first and second trimesters and celebrated the news with everyone. On April 17th, we were six months pregnant, and the fertility specialist was elated that our darling baby boy was resting happily inside my belly. We celebrated by buying more baby stuff. Only three more months and he would be home. The next day, our son was dead.

I remember everything like it was yesterday. I had this sudden urge to go to the bathroom. When I sat on the toilet, I could not stop peeing, but it did not feel like peeing. It felt like something I had never felt before. I was on the phone with my girlfriend and told her I felt like I was peeing forever, but it did not feel normal. She told me to go to the doctor and get checked because it sounded like my water broke. I did not believe her, but I called my mom, and we went to the doctor to ensure everything was okay. It was not okay. A few hours later, I found myself hooked up to machines in the hospital. The pain started mild but soon got so excruciating I wanted to pull my teeth out. My mom kept reassuring me that I was not going into labor because the machines were not showing any contractions. The sharp pain went on for hours. Eventually, the pain was unbearable, and I felt the only way to get relief was going to the bathroom. I made my way to the bathroom and sat on the toilet. I remember feeling like I had huge bowel movement coming from my vagina. I could not understand what was happening until I put my hands between my legs and pulled him to the front of me. I had given birth to my son in the hospital's toilet, lifeless in my hands.

"Don't let my family come in!" I remember screaming as I hit the nurse button next to the toilet. The bathroom was no longer a soft, warm grey but a dark red as blood swallowed the toilet, the floor, and every step taken back to my hospital bed. After a D&C (dilation and curettage), loss of blood circulation below my waist, loss of color in my lips, and three blood transfusions, the doctors realized that the nurse had never attached the contraction monitor. That was the reason no one understood why I kept saying I was in so much pain. I was in labor the entire time. All these doctors and nurses were around me, but no one realized I was giving birth to my son, Justin.

I went to see him. They wrapped him in a blue blanket, and my husband and I held him. We did not say a word. Justin already looked like him. He had all his dad's facial features. How could the specialist congratulate me on a healthy six-month pregnancy on Tuesday, and on Wednesday, Justin was gone? It was almost unbearable. We took his blanket, a card with his footprints, and other keepsakes from the hospital. We never said a word.

The day we buried Justin, we buried our marriage too. Nothing was ever the same after that. I was so depressed that I started self-medicating and sleeping a lot. I remember the most beautiful dreams when I would sleep. I would go to this world where I could see Justin playing and smiling, and I could always be with him. It was magical. He always looked happy running in the fields of flowers and mesmerized by the kites flying in the air. I remember one moment, watching him play through the window as I laid his clothes out for the next day. He was so happy and so was I. I wanted to go to sleep so much that I didn't want to wake up one day. I remember going to Baby Land and sitting at his tombstone. For some reason, I felt closer to him there. I would lay down on the ground with my ear resting in the dirt, trying to see if I could hear him. Being with him seemed to have become an obsession. So much so that I decided to get a gun, go to his grave, and end my life at his tombstone. Our blood would once again unite - this time in death.

Chapter Four

Ashes to Ashes

Growing up, I was always afraid of death. Perhaps because my mom told me that death was the one thing I would have to do alone. That concept was difficult to absorb. To know that one day, I would go to sleep and not wake up was terrifying! I did not sleep for days after that. It seemed like death was a punishment for being born. After hearing so many negative things about death, I started to feel like the fear of death was more powerful than death itself. I wondered if having people so frightened of dying was not a power move for people to control emotions and behaviors. I couldn't count the times people told me I could only have a peaceful death if I followed everything they said in a little black book or their ideology. To top it off, they told me I didn't need to read the black book and that I could not ask questions.

For a while, I followed suit and tried to do everything I could to guarantee a triumphant death. But soon, it became difficult to follow arbitrary rules while contradictions stared me in the face. Once I matured, I began reading and exploring the concept of dying. Ironically, the day I decided to go against the masses and raise my hand was when I started not to fear death. I finally accepted with peace that it was the one thing I could not escape.

This moment doesn't seem real
Having to say my final goodbye
Always pretended to be strong
But today, I can't even try

Life starts ending when it begins
But I am grateful we had our time
Death has memories of you now
But it could never take away mine

Words are running through my head
And I'm not sure where I should start
See when Fate stepped into our paths
Something powerful pierced my heart

It runs deeper than deep and on
This love that I have for you
Though pain ricochets my body
I know what you'd say to do

Hold on to what is pure
And love and love over again
One day, Death will have memories of you
And you will rest with me, my friend

My grandmother was vibrant and enjoyed life enough for three or four people. There was so much about her to love. I loved that she always dressed for more than the occasion. It was never the wrong time to be fabulously stunning. Even if it were a family dinner, you can bet she would be dripping in her diamonds, wearing a long flowing wig, and sashaying in a dress that embraced all her Coca-Cola bottle-shaped curves. She was the same way on the church usher board, too. When I think of her as the only usher decked out in gold chains, big earrings, and diamond bracelets, I cannot help but smile. She would attend church with her white uniform, stylish glasses with jewels hanging, and a glow that could melt butter in the winter. She was beautiful inside and out. And good heavens above, could she cook? When I say cook, I do not mean, like me, cooking coffee and boiled eggs. My grandma's food would have you slapping yourself and anyone else within a five-mile radius. Her favorite things in life were cooking for her family, serving on the usher board, and being the life of the party. Oh, and I could never forget fishing.

One summer, she promised my cousins we would go camping in her RV. We were excited to spend a few days in a fully loaded, air-conditioned RV, pretending we were camping in the wild! The night before heading out, she said if we let her go fishing first, she would take us camping for a day longer. We were like, "Okay, bet! Surely, fishing won't take that long." The next day, we woke up at 2:00 am, heading to her favorite fishing spot three hours away. We slept all the way, determined to save all our energy for camping. When we woke up, it was sunrise, and my grandmother was singing and yelling, "We are here!" We crawled out of the car, yawning and complaining. It was hot and muddy, and there was hardly any shade to shelter from the sun. I am unaware of the individual who conceptualized fishing as an enjoyable activity, but we hated it.

But grandma loved every moment with her big sun hat on, baiting her hook, and grinning. After being there for seven hours, we realized we were not going camping at all! Oh, my goodness, we were furious. We sat on that muddy ground, cussing and grumbling while eating sweaty bologna sandwiches. We vowed never to speak to her again. She finished fishing one hundred hours later and had the nerve to ask us if we had fun! We just looked at her. But my grandma could have cared less as she held her bucket of fresh fish in her arms and skipped to the car.

There were so many memorable moments. The day she died, a part of me died too. We were so much alike. It was hard seeing her in such a debilitating state after she was diagnosed with cancer. Sometimes, I would go into her room; all I saw was the white of her eyes. I could not tell whether she was with me or had crossed over to the other side. I remember her crying, and we asked her what was wrong. She said she would never see us again. It broke my heart. I listened as the family assured her that was untrue and how much we loved her. She crossed over shortly after that moment.

> *I see the tears roll down your face*
> *As you whisper your last goodbye*
> *If you knew the peace that embraced my soul*
> *My love, you would not cry*

> *Tomorrow, for me no more will come*
> *And to many, that's a final farewell*
> *But now I know the beauties untold*
> *That on your side, no man can tell*

> *The path I traveled was hard at times*
> *And it seemed I was walking alone*
> *But when I reached heaven, I knew*
> *I had finally made it home*

When Justin died, I was devastated at how small the casket was. It seemed so against nature that a child would leave this world alone in a white coffin. I nearly passed out. People came and held me up, telling me to be strong. Immediately I became confused about what the fuck and who the fuck I was to be strong for in front of my son's coffin. If there was a time to be weak and succumb to grief, it had to be when you were burying your child! When I got to my seat, I was fixated on opening the casket to see if he had woken up. I saw shows in which people had done it before. But instead, I just sat there in a daze as I looked and still felt pregnant.

We had a small program right next to Baby Land. Seeing the angel statue watching over the babies somehow brought me peace. At first, the rain and wind were brutal during the ceremony. I remember thinking that all the raindrops in the world could not compare to how much my heart wept. And then suddenly, the rain stopped, the sun came out, and the birds started to sing. My husband went to the car and got all the balloons we bought for Justin. As we released the balloons and they floated into the sky, I whispered, "Rest now with the angels."

One thing I thought about night after night was hearing my dad give the blessings at the ceremony and saying, "We thank God for Justin." I am not sure why that resonated with me. I suppose because my dad always taught me to give thanks in all things. He lived it, which was more important than teaching it. I was too broken, though, to say thank you. I had so many questions that required answers. There were so many rotten to the core adults that death could have chosen to snatch instead of my son. He could have lived.

A year later, I tried going to church on Mother's Day, but I could not stomach the "Would All the Mothers Stand Up" presentation. It just reminded me that I could and should have been a mother. Instead, I went to Justin's grave. Once parked by Baby Land, I cried so hard I could not move. A man in a suit knocking on my car window interrupted me. When I rolled down the window, he handed me a card-like thing and said, "Happy Mother's Day." I burst out weeping so loudly it sounded like echoes through the wind. When I got myself together, I pulled out the card. It started, "To Mothers of Babies in Baby Land." I sat crying, holding that card close to my heart. That was one of the best Mother's Day I ever had. Over time, I found more strength. I started focusing on living a life that Justin would be proud of. I will always cherish how extraordinary it felt to have him inside me. For that, I am thankful.

Daddy once told me about this freedom
When I was too young to comprehend
About a man who could say "Walkthrough"
When circumstances said it's the end

I was brokenhearted and wanted to let go
But for some reason I did not fall
Not knowing that the man Daddy knew
Had carried me through it all

Oblivious to the pain that was in store
And the obstacles impeding my way
He'd quiet the angry beast of destruction
And in the midst I was safe to stay

This freedom you taught me Daddy
Sustained me through my walk of strife
I was finally able to find peace Daddy
When Death took Justin's life

Free at last free at last
I can hear the angels sing
Restored to live life again
With the peace that freedom brings

Chapter Five

Loving Betrayal

If I can't feel your heart next to my breast
If I can't feel your touch or tender caress
If I can't cook your dinner or play around
If I can't help mold this love we found
If I can't rock you to sleep or hold you near
If I can't hear you say it or cradle your fear
What this does to me how can I explain
Surviving off memories isn't the same

"Wake up. Wake up," someone whispered in my ear. It startled me straight out of my sleep. When I opened my eyes, no one was there. It was Wednesday at 1:30 am, and as usual, I had taken sleeping pills to fight my insomnia. I reached across the bed and realized my husband had not come home. During the week, he usually got home around midnight after working the night shift. Wait, is that him in the bathroom? He was in the shower humming a song. In another bedroom, I heard his phone go off simultaneously. I got up, went to the other bedroom, and did something I had never done in the five years we were married: I answered the phone, "Hello." There was silence. Oh well, I thought it was the wrong number. So, I hung up. I was leaving the room when his phone pinged with a text. The text read, "I just called, and I think your wife answered the phone. I think she knows." There was no name under contacts, but there were countless messages. I thought, "No wonder he is singing; he's seeing some chic on the side. She should know not to call him at 1:30 am."

I scrolled through the messages...

"I had a great time last night."

"Where are we meeting for lunch today?"

"See you at the gym."

"Thinking of you."

"Your wife is such a bitch."

"Look at you with your dance moves."

"I can't wait to see you and miss you."

"I enjoyed being on the yacht with you. That was so much fun."

"Your wife is a dumb bitch. She is so stupid."

"There is nothing wrong with you loving me. It is natural for two men to say that they love each other."

"I love you and miss you."

I stopped reading and stood there frozen for a minute. I was in shock! These messages were not from a woman, but rather from a man to my husband. "What the fuck!" I called the number back, and the voice said, "Hello." It was a man! It felt like an out-of-body experience. I said, "Hello, this is your boyfriend's wife." There was silence and then he hung up. I went into the bathroom, where my husband was finishing his shower, still humming! I immediately started screaming at the top of my lungs, "Your boyfriend just called, and I talked to him. I also saw the fucking text messages of him calling me a bitch and you two saying I love you! What the fuck!" My husband looked like a deer caught in headlights. I threw his phone at him and said, "Call the motherfucker back now!"

At first, we went back and forth, but then he finally agreed. I told him, "When you call his ass, put him on speaker and do not say shit about me being here." I think that phone did not have a chance to even ring when dude picked it up. All my husband said was, "Hello" and as soon as he realized it was him on the other end the dude began singing like a freed bird who had been in bondage for forty years. I believe the song he sang went something like this, "You were right; your wife is a bitch. A stupid bitch at that (he laughed). I called you, but she answered and then called me back. But don't worry; I didn't say anything. I just hung up on her ass (he laughed). Fuck that stupid whore, who cares

46

if she knows? There is nothing wrong with our relationship. There is nothing wrong with two men having the relationship we do. It is very natural." My husband was dead silent. But the dumb dumb on the other end did not even realize my husband's hesitance to speak, and he kept singing. "I do love you and hope we see each other again soon. Tonight was so much fun! Don't worry about that bitch." It was at that moment I unleashed! Every word was a curse word, and I ended my monologue in a calm before the storm voice telling him, "If you ever call me a bitch or a whore again, I will cut your fucking ass into small pieces. Better yet, since you know so much about me, I dare you - no, I invite you to come to my house and call me a bitch in the face. Please call me a bitch in my face!" For three minutes, my husband, his boyfriend, and I said nothing. Then I said, "Bye bitch!" and hung up.

I began shouting at my husband, claiming that I could not believe he was gay. He said absolutely nothing at all. I packed up some clothes and said I was going to my parents. As I opened the door to the garage, something told me to go back. I closed the door and went back to our bedroom. This shit cannot be real! This is absurd! My husband was in our bed on the phone with this dude, asking him if he was okay! What in the world is going on!? I started screaming all over again. I could not believe he was on the phone with this dude while I was leaving crying and confused, and he did nothing to console me. I told him I was taking an AIDS test, and we were done. All I kept thinking about was my friend's aunt, whose husband was secretly with men and gave her HIV. She died and that bastard lived forever and a day. I was numb. My husband did not move. He did not chase me. He did not hug me. He did not apologize. He did not do anything. My husband, as I knew him, was dead at that moment. I did not recognize the man before me.

I drove away in a fog. Tears blurred my vision as I went to the only place I knew to find solace: my parents' home. I sat there looking at my watch and it wasn't even 6 am. I didn't want to disrupt their sleep on a weekday. So, I drove to a gas station and waited a while. So many thoughts were going through my head, but it was like in a language I did not understand. The only thing I did understand was that no one could comfort me like my mom and dad.

When I got to their gate again, I did not care what time it was. Thankfully, I still had a gate opener. I let myself in and drove up their driveway. Very calmly, I buzzed the doorbell and pushed the intercom button to say, "Mom, can I come in?" When I got upstairs, they looked at me and asked, "Is everything okay?" I yelled, "He is gay!" and burst out weeping. They were like, "Who is gay?" I screamed, "My husband!" I fell to my knees so hard, sobbing, that I thought the ceiling would cave in. They stood there absorbing what I said for a moment and then went to hug me. I curled up in a ball on the floor and yelled, "Don't touch me! I have to take an AIDS test." I cried even harder. They said they did not care about any AIDS test and hugged me so tight that it felt like I was a child again.

> When I'm down and out, and the world is cold
> When words go unspoken, and silence gets old
> When the lies I've heard have no beginning nor end
> I can lean on my rock, my family, and friend
>
> When the life I live is so full of grief
> When the path I take wreaks havoc, not peace
> When I have no reason to keep the faith within
> I can lean on my rock, my family, and friend
>
> When the smiles I greet seem a prelude to death
> When the flesh is weak, and all I see is self
> When the love I've given blindsides me with revenge
> I can lean on my rock, my family, and friend
>
> When I overcome the darkness, it is clear in the light
> The shoulder I leaned on didn't weaken through the fight
> What we have is something rare and precious among men
> To be able to say family and in the same breath, friend

That day was a turning point for me and my marriage. I never thought it would be a man calling. If it were a woman, most women would know how to deal with the situation, but if it were a man, what do you do? I started reminiscing about signs I may have missed or if there had been a change in his behavior. If there was one, it had to have been subtle.

We never pried in each other's lives nor acted like we owned each other. Our relationship was a marriage and a friendship. I was more disappointed in the friendship part than the marriage. He could have shared his struggles with me as friends. Hell, maybe it wasn't a struggle for him, but it was for me. Damn him for letting me go through this bullshit. It was unforgivable.

I was sweating profusely and could not feel my heartbeat waiting at the doctor's office. Suddenly, the nurse came out and yelled my name. I must have been in a fog because I did not hear her say it the first two times. As I walked towards her and headed to the doctor's room, signs were plastered all over the walls about HIV and AIDS. I thought I was going to throw up my insides. "Mam, what can we do for you today," the nurse asked. I whispered through tears, "I need an AIDS and HIV test, please." Of course, that was her cue to get all curious, as if we were on the Jerry Springer Show. "Oh, I see. So, what makes you think you have been exposed? Were you having sex unprotected with multiple partners?" she asked. "No. I just found out my husband has a boyfriend," I whispered.

Someone came in and took so much blood that I thought the nurse had to be a vampire. I couldn't tell if my blood was infected in the tubes, but I was trying to see. At the same time, I did not want to think about it. "Okay, that is all we need for now. You will be getting a call in about three days with the results," she said. With my head still down, I smiled slightly and left. The next few days were bombarded with the groundwork of protecting others if I were positive and what I could or could not do anymore. I had three days to plan. A few days later, I got the call. The nurse started, "Mam, we have your results for the AIDS and HIV test. Is it okay for me to give it over the phone?" I replied, "Yes." She continued, "Your tests returned negative, but you will still need to test routinely." I was relieved. Thank goodness both were negative. That was one positive thing that came out of this chaos. But because he never asked about the results, my husband would never know.

What do you do when time runs out
When the one you love leaves you alone
Yea, his body may lay with you at night
But his heart is no longer at home

How does it feel when you give and give
In the end, you get nothing in return
Life can be full of countless lessons
But life doesn't force you to learn

Where do you go when his arms are free
From holding the one who always cares
The clock is slowly ticking away
And for you, he is no longer there

When will you see this road is a "U"
You are headed straight for a brick wall
What, when, where, and how tell half
But your emptiness tells it all

Chapter Six

Raging Calm

I left the house we shared and moved in with my family. While I sat in the confines of four walls, he was out kicking it with his boyfriend. They spent $1,000 from our joint account in one night. Then, the next night, an added few hundred dollars at a strip club. As I watched our coins fund his newly found freedom festivities, I was overwhelmed. I had lost my son. Now, I was losing my husband.

Seeing him at the bank weeks later to separate our bank accounts seemed oddly familiar. He was protective, caring, and graciously kind. I remember him asking how I was doing, and I just looked at him. He did not look the same. His dress and mannerisms were different. He wore open-toe Jesus sandals, had a cute sag in his jeans, and walked a little loose around the hips. I tried to concentrate on the reason for our reunion rather than him appearing as though he could outdo me twisting through the bank. This scenario could not be part of my life. Who was this guy?

Over the next few weeks, he assured me that he loved me. So, we decided to talk about it. We began seeing a psychologist separately, then together. But during one of our joint sessions, the psychologist told me I could not ask questions about my husband's other life, what he did, or the guy. I was livid. I shouted, "I just want my husband back as he used to be." The psychologist looked at me and said, "That person is dead."

You want someone to hold you, but all you have is what's inside
You swallow the sour taste of rejection and comfort it with pride
You wish he understood the truth without you speaking a word
But the indignity of self-pity roaring is the only sound he heard
You jumped into it, eyes glazed shut, not seeing what was ahead
Believing it'll work out for the good, but heartache came instead
You'll learn true love is loving yourself; you can be whole again
When you love the person who's inside, real love will never end

After more counseling and self-reflection, I found the strength to accept my new reality. It was not easy. Part of me wanted to stay married because I knew something was going on inside my husband and thought I could fix it. I was so confused. Infidelity has never taken me to the mindset of ending a marriage, but this shit right here was something I never contemplated. Regardless, I wanted to try at least to understand. I was not ready for it, but I was willing to talk. Unfortunately, the more we were around each other, the more he hated me.

He went from being gentle, supportive, thoughtful, and considerate to being abusive. The abuse intensified every time I was in his space. I remember going by our home to pick up clothes. He was working in the front yard. Neither one of us spoke as I went inside. He was not even supposed to be there. Oh well. When I returned to my truck, I rolled down the window so we could talk. Suddenly, he started yelling, "Get out of here!" I said, "What? What is wrong with you? This shit is not my fault!" He walked up to the driver's side window, and his eyes looked filled with blood as he reared back with his fist. I sped off in shock. He had never behaved that way before. He had never hit me.

Nonetheless, the verbal abuse escalated to the point of no return. His words were like venom from the deadliest place in hell. I was baffled. It was as though he had pure disdain for me.

When finalizing our divorce, I remember telling him that divorce was the hardest thing ever. He said, "No, losing my son was." I looked into his eyes, and that was when I found out the truth. He had never mentioned our son after he died, until now. It was clear that every time he saw me, it reminded him that I was the vessel that deprived him of his firstborn. I constantly reminded him of the pain he felt, which he kept bottled up inside. So he found solace in someone who could never bring him that kind of pain again.

I grieved for us. Our misplaced anger and bitterness consumed all that was once good and treasured. We had become enemies. I was self-medicating and battling insomnia. He was insulting and dismissive of our vows. Violence, threats of destruction, and financial squandering were all we had left.

One night, he called at some ungodly hour, asking what I was doing. He questioned if I had sent a spirit to our home to visit him because one came to the foot of the bed. I assured him I did not send a ghost and was asleep. He said if I did not do it, someone from my family or close to me did, and I was in danger. He needed to protect me and ward off evil spirits. A few days later, he invited me to the house to talk. Unbeknownst to me, he had visited a witch doctor who made him a concoction that looked like a bunch of spices. I asked, "What is this? Is this what you wanted to discuss?" He said, "Someone has put a spell on you, and you must have this on you at all times to protect you from evil spirits." He held the aluminum foil with the spices in the air, prayed over it, and started his protection ritual. He sprinkled the concoction under my car mat, in the glove compartment, in the sole of the shoes I had on, in my purse, literally everywhere. He even had it all over the house. It was ridiculous to me, but I did not push back. Unbeknownst to me, that situation was nothing compared to what would come.

It soon became clear that my husband had multiple personalities, and one of them hated me. The other one blamed me for not feeding him when he was hungry as a child. We were cleaning the garage one day, and I asked what he wanted for dinner. He looked at me and said, "So now you want to feed me! You knew I was hungry and didn't give me anything." I was not sure what was happening. "When were you hungry? I do not remember you asking for food and me saying no," I questioned with a confused look. His eyes were frustrated as he yelled, "You know when! I told you I was hungry when it happened, and you did not give me anything. I was the only child with no food." Trying to convince him that I did not know him as a child and that it was not me was terrifying. The longer I denied it, the closer he got to my face. He kept calling me some other woman's name, who was his aunt, and getting more upset. Seeing him so adamant that I was her forced me to become her. I apologized for not feeding him when he was younger and asked if I could make it up to him by getting him any food he wanted at any time. Then he told me what he wanted for dinner.

One of the most troubling incidents happened when we were in bed together. I woke up to him staring at me with a blank look. It was his body, but his countenance and spirit were someone else, someone evil. I asked if he was okay. He did not say a word. He just looked at me. I told him I loved him and waited for him to lie down and sleep. When he did, I laid down, but no rest was in my future.

I can still see his face staring at me. That was the first time I experienced seeing another person literally in someone's body. The following day, I mustered up the courage to ask him what was happening last night when he was staring at me. He said, "I do not know what you are talking about. I do not remember staring or speaking to you last night." I simply smiled and replied, "Oh, that's fine."

The professionals were right; he could have killed me that night. Two psychologists told me that I was lucky to be alive. I remember one doctor explicitly telling me that I was in danger because one of my husband's personalities wanted me dead, which was profoundly serious. He also warned that I should not speak to my husband when he was in that mental state because it would not be my husband; I would be talking to someone else. I knew it was true.

Shortly after that warning, my husband told people he would kill me and my parents. His ominous desires frightened someone so much that the man came to warn us. I did not even know him. He was terrified as he shared details of the plot to see us all dead. It was unbelievable, but he couldn't have known some of my family's details unless my husband told him. I knew it was true.

The next day, I printed the paperwork for my life insurance policy. When the beneficiary updates were official, I gave a copy to my mom. She started crying. I was so detached from my emotions that I did not shed one tear. I assured her I would let him kill me before anything happened to them. From that moment forward, I always carried pepper spray, a knife, and a gun. Even after the divorce, I slept with a loaded gun on my nightstand.

His family knew about his history of mental peril but never shared or warned me about it. I called them repeatedly, begging them to call me when my husband was out of control and threatening to kill me. They never did. These people had the same blood through their veins as my husband, but they acted as if nothing was happening. They never reached out to me during those tumultuous times or after our divorce. It was as though they did not know me at all. Maybe they were just as scared as I was, but they could have at least called. I will never forgive them.

My marriage eventually ended one Thanksgiving weekend. I will never forget it. His tongue was so full of disgust as he told me he hated me, called me a pathetic bitch, and left. I can still see the clothes spread in the laundry room doorway leading to the garage. I spent that holiday alone and didn't call or tell anyone. I thought he picked that moment because he knew my family was out of town and no one could comfort me. I remember sitting on the cold hardwood floor by the fireplace, crying the entire Thanksgiving holiday. There was nothing for me to be thankful for.

You constantly say I am holding you
Like a bird that wants to be free
But when the storms of life get rocky
For your stillness, you come to me

Day after day, depleting my source
Without any replenishment in sight
Running the streets is priority #1
No consciousness of wrong or right

Remember who shared your deepest woes
And stood by you even when alone
Lies penetrating your deceiving grin
And the same lies keep you from home

You once protected me and I felt safe
You even encouraged me to be bold
But now you despise the woman you see
Instead of wanting to make her whole

Three months later, we were divorced. It was tough to describe the roller coaster of emotions I experienced. My heart screamed, "DO NOT RESUSCITATE!" Life broke me into a gazillion pieces. My most disturbing memory during the marriage was feeling so emotionally and mentally drained that I went around looking like a zombie. I remember leaving the house with no shoes, clothes that did not match, and hair all over my head. It was like I was watching myself and trying to talk to myself, but simultaneously, I could not hear myself. Nothing seemed real. I had become so consumed with grief and trauma that I felt I could not live anymore. I was already dead to myself.

I remember telling my husband how I was feeling during that time. I also remember him saying that if I committed suicide, he would throw Jazz in the river. Jazz was our fur baby (dog), a miniature pinscher. He got her for me six months into dating. When we parted ways, I remember Jazz waiting by the garage door for him to come home from work. I would tell her that he was gone, and it was just us. But she still waited for weeks. I allowed her to experience her heartache. I cannot count the nights she cuddled with me as I experienced mine.

Chapter Seven

Insatiable Thirst

I started graduate school two weeks after my divorce. Something about turning that pain into inspiration worked for me. All my energy was wrapped into working full-time, learning, reading, and writing. There was no time left for grief, or even sleep. As long as I pretended, life was great. I even started dating again. I'm not sure if you'd call it dating. It was more of my attempt to feel beautiful and desired by a man. Meeting someone was never a problem, and it happened without effort.

Dieone had a calm presence, was easy on the eyes, and had a rich country dialect mixed with a New York accent. When we met, I knew there was not any future with him. But that was fine with me. I was only trying to survive the present. When he looked at me, he knew my body needed to be ravished, pressure unleashed, and things taken beyond average lubriciousness. He treated me and my golden locket like queens. Even though sex was exhilarating, it stopped being gratifying at some point. There is a difference between sex and making love. It felt great when he wrapped his hand around my neck while pinning me to the hotel wall as my body screamed. But as soon as he was done, so was I. Nothing lingered. I did not want to cuddle, be touched, or even have a conversation. I just wanted him to leave. He served his purpose. It was just a moment, a moment I tried to forget.

Not wanting to travel the same road twice
But this path seems so deja vu
The last time here wasn't that long
And this shit doesn't smell brand new

Listening to hormones instead of my heart
A quiet storm awakens within
The radio enticing my body's desires
A stunning start to a lack luster end

I should have said no and just walked away
Because my heart was tired of the game
Drained from lust's superficial cravings
But the rest of me wanted the pain

So, I pretended for a moment I was free
But the pleasure I felt was soon gone
The reality denied was still waiting for me
A prisoner to shackles unknown

I have always longed to share every part of me emotionally and intimately. During my marriage, I could only go so far. He complained I wanted to have sex too much. Seriously, is that possible? Wanting to have sex at least twice a day seemed more than reasonable. If I could have sex as much as I wanted, it would be three times a day, with weekend shut-ins every other week. I have always been sensual, and it metamorphosed into being sexual too. I remember wanting my panty and bra to match early on in life. No one saw it, but something about it made me feel feminine. There wasn't one night that my ex-husband saw me not wearing something sexy to bed. I was doing that even when I was not married or seeing anyone. Something about lace and silk against my skin made me feel sublime.

It is funny when I think back. All the things marriage books and people told me would turn a husband on (e.g., lingerie, dressing appealing, keeping yourself up, etc.) I did, and then some. Sure, it got his attention, but not in a profoundly passionate sexual way. I never felt he enjoyed sex as thoroughly as I did. But somehow, he made me feel so beautiful. Even with that, there were parts of him I could not reach. I think he felt it, too. But we were happy as friends, and I was always free to be my wild, funny, crazy self.

A few months after Dieone, I ventured into online dating. It was a tidal wave of entertainment that was dipped, rolled, and deep-fried into a chaotic mess. The most annoying part was posting multiple pictures including an entire body shot, to have men ask for more. "Help me understand the point of putting pictures on my profile so you can ask for some anyway?" I would ask. The most common response was wanting a picture to add to my name in their phone. I couldn't have cared less if they had listed me as unknown. Goodness, grief!

I was speaking to multiple guys on the phone. It was nothing major, mainly small talk. One guy, Mr. Screensaver, and I talked on the phone for only a few days when he told me his coworkers said I was pretty. I was like, oh, okay. "So, how did they see my picture?" I asked. He responded, "Because it is on my screensaver at work." I replied, "Oh, okay," how weird. I told him I did not understand why he would have my picture as his screensaver at work or anywhere since we had never met and only spoken on the phone for a few days. Plus, he didn't even know if that was me in the picture. He replied, "I have prayed for a special woman and God told me it was you. I do not care how you look. I care about your soul, and I am already in love with it. I know we were meant to be, so I am living in that assurance." BLOCKED.

Then came proposals, threesomes, BDSM (bondage, discipline, dominance, submission, and sadism), and other unsolicited invites. But that was nothing compared to one guy, who was sweet as pie but insisted that our first date be at his place so he could cook me dinner. I told him that that was not how I envisioned dating. He was suspiciously persistent. Eventually, I got him to divulge why he wanted me to come over for dinner. He said he wanted me to come over so he could tie me up to his bed, blindfold me, and sexually explore every orifice of my body. I did not respond right away. Nor was I in shock. But I did sit there momentarily, envisioning him as Hannibal Lecter with an apron on, cooking and smiling as he planned my fate. People have various exploration levels of sex; I get that. But Mr. Hannibal did not even know my government name, and he had no confirmation that I was the person in the pictures. As I sipped my old-fashioned, I said, "Thank you for being honest. Always be honest to avoid wasting time and increase your chances of finding someone who can fulfill your desires. That said, I am fairly sure we are not a match."

That was wild, but I expected it since I was an avid ID channel watcher. The scenarios on all those shows had me extra cautious. That was why going on dates was far and in between for me. But if I did go on a date, I would include a picture of his license, license plate number, and current photo in my information packet to my girlfriend. Who, by the way, would be watching in the bushes. Yep, either in the bushes watching or sitting at a table close by. It may sound extreme, but dating online has brought out some characters.

There were some cool guys, too. Some of them just wanted to wine and dine for companionship. One guy took me to a nice restaurant, where a violinist came by our table to perform. It was so sweet. Unfortunately, it reminded him of his ex because it is where they used to go!!! He cried the entire date over his ex-girlfriend. I just listened while ordering another bottle of wine. At the end of the date, we stood together feeling the Carolina breeze while I encouraged him to give her a call. I understood the struggle of loving someone and trying to progress without them. It is good to be there for people because sometimes we all have different motivations for dating. Heck, I was in the same boat. I was not online opening my heart up for love; I was just there to hear I was pretty and desired. My genius attempt at putting a bandage on a wound that needed stitches. Nothing more and nothing less.

I told myself there's no need to cry
But fighting tears seems hard to bear
When you left you took a part of me
My heart never knew was there

Now that it is gone a hollow space
Left me aging inside of my soul
The one I loved and cherished most
His betrayal is now taking a toll

My face is smiling a frown upside down
No one knows the pain I go through
But one day, you'll feel what it's like to love
Someone who could never love you

This letter I write is my final goodbye
In time another chapter shall begin
Cremating your love and walking away
Let your ashes pollute the wind

Memories of you painfully forged
Will no longer have a place in the end
My mind and soul are being revived
Let the beauty of resurrection begin

The struggle to find self-worth after such a traumatic time was exhausting. Many times, I did what I needed to do just to be okay. Even if life was a lie tripled dipped in temporary gratification. It sustained me for the moment, and all I had was that moment. I was holding on to a string when it came to self-esteem. I looked shiny and well put together but was scared and tattered inside. I was lost. I acknowledge that. I admit and accept that I made poor choices in order to feel valued. But I did not let those decisions bombard my brain. It was necessary to tread the murky waters of depression and self-harm. Physical touch and affirmation have always been my top love languages, and I was on a journey of creating a universe that supplied me with both.

One night, I was at home, soaking my face in tears and processing my divorce, when some of my down-to-ride-anytime cousins stopped by. I emerged from the door with a sloppy, crooked wig. They just looked at me and shook their heads. Finally, they said, "You need some vitamin D." Well dang! It appeared that their liquid courage and natural aromatic plant intake gave them ESP. That sounded great. But when I got married, I had destroyed all of my little black books and had no prospects. But that did not deter them. Before I knew it, we were all in the car and headed to the store. We pulled into the parking lot, giggling nonstop like silly underage kids going to Magic Springs without their parent's permission.

We had not entered the door well when the lady behind the counter asked if we wanted to enter the room. I said, "The room. I don't understand." However, my uninhibited cousin understood. He responded, "Oh, that is the room where you watch porn and can have sex." I immediately told the woman, "No, mam. We are all family!" Why did the woman look like that did not matter, and why was she still waiting for an answer? I seriously had no comment. We just laughed and started going down the aisles.

Some people led me to believe that a sex store was Satan's den, where he did his bidding for souls. That was so far from being true. At least, I did not think it was confirmed based on the happy feelings and biting of my bottom lip I did while exploring. My cousins must have picked up at least twenty vibrators, read instructions, and compared intensity levels. They were determined that I would get something one way or another, even if it were manufactured.

Once we decided on the length of my blessings, we paid for them and left. When we returned to my place, we took a few shots and talked about how much fun I would have once they went home. But before they left, they told me to make sure I gave the vibrator receipt to my divorce attorney so my ex could pay for it! I love my cousins for showing up and showing out that night. I promised to try my new friend and let them know how it went. That night was one of the best healing nights during my divorce. At that moment, I realized divorce did not have to equate to misery.

It took me a few days to get to know my new friend. For maximum enjoyment, I read the instructions in English, as well as the parts in Spanish that I understood. I got myself some energizer batteries in the value pack, picked up a box of candles, and then was ready! I turned on some music and retired to bed, and my goodness! My new blessing was hitting spots that had been neglected for a long minute. It felt so good I took a break and called my cousin. I had to tell her all about it! Yep, it was that amazing. My body needed that relief. After that night, I did not need a fortune teller to look into her crystal ball and tell me about my future. It was clear that sex stores and sex toys would be part of my life forever.

Chapter Eight

Perfect Misfit

I was told I was not normal
And that I should ask for grace
Being a lady means dignity
And sensuality has no place

You sound like a sneaky whore
You certainly need some help
Like the woman at the well
You are the reason Jesus wept

Wait, it is all figured out
How you can sin no more
Cast this demon back to hell
In hell's fire let him roar

You can still be redeemed
Even though you went astray
Now join me for redemption
For repentance we shall pray

Unlike society's ridicule, I have always felt that sexuality, sensuality, and intimacy were a natural part of existence. I never felt sex was terrible or should only be whispered about in the dark when no one was around. Why was it so wrong to say, "I ENJOY SEX!" There was a lot wrong with saying that; for starters, you would probably be considered a nympho, which isn't too bad if you knew the definition. The definition of a nympho is someone who has strong sexual desires. That does not sound deviant to me. However, society makes it sound like you are as filthy as ten alley cats. That's far from the truth. It just means that you enjoy making your body moan with pleasure. That isn't a sin.

Being intrigued and curious about my body came naturally. In my twenties, I had a special friend who got so much pleasure from feasting. I always wondered why "my person" would feast on my body from evening to sunrise. I once took a moment to become acquainted with my chocolate glory, and it was a damn sight! Oh, my goodness! I finally understood everything. My scent was erotic and alluring. It even made me blush.

I smell you
An aphrodisiac I adore
Just thinking
Why enough for me means more

Eyes closed
Concentrate on how I feel
Just waiting
To touch and purr at will

Sip slow
Enjoying how it tastes
Just thankful
Every drop has its place

No words
Show instead of tell
Just know
My lips throb as well

Right there
Feeling what I said
Just wishing
I was her instead

It was not too long after that experience when I realized I could get aroused without touching myself. Not only that, but I could have an orgasm without touching myself. That was amazing to me. Sometimes, the orgasmic intensity would be so strong that my glory walls would ache for days. Other times, it felt so good that I would do it multiple times a day, anywhere, and anytime. I once told my girlfriend that I had pleasured myself while watching

Maury. She was like, "Maury, who?" I said, "Maury Povich! You know the lie detector says that is a lie." A brief silence followed a pause. Then she said, "BBBIIITTTTCHHHHHH!" That was the longest bitch anyone ever called me in my life. I still laugh aloud when I think about it. The real humor is that I did not see why having a "happy ending" watching the results of a pregnancy test or the evening news was so awkward. Any time was the right time to enjoy a moment. That quality made for a euphoric sexual experience that I eagerly welcomed into my life.

I felt dominant and began to master the ability to climax alone. The best part is that I could experience gratification without worrying about someone trying to hug me after sex and asking to spend the night. For many moons, I was never into cuddling after sex. I just wanted to shower and go to bed without getting groped all night and having someone beg for more. When I think about it, I have only felt like snuggling after sex with one person. It wasn't in my twenties, and it wasn't with my ex-husband. Perhaps I was saving that part of myself for someone who would accept all of me. However, that person arrived later in life. Until then, I was thrilled with exploring the power of mental and sexual pleasure, which was the most potent intimacy of all. Making love to someone without touching was the ultimate indicator that you had achieved something more profound than just sex.

While married, I accepted whatever married sex life resembled. I was going to hang in there as much as possible. Even before marriage, I could never express my sexual desires, so marriage was an unfortunate continuation of sexual frustration. To release some of the tension, I wrote about it and imagined it in my dreams. The most riveting and uninhibited version of me was Velvet Sin. She was courageous, captivating, intriguing, and confident. She anticipated the invitation for sex and never felt guilty or apologized for being true. The only problem is that she only lived between my paper and pen.

Her thoughts and desires were way beyond the average missionary style of doing things. She understood but was not concerned that her actual sexual peak would be shunned and looked upon as deviant. Some would even consider it an absolute dishonor for a woman to want an animalistic entanglement while still considering herself a lady. How shameful! But the silk, chocolate, smooth, and uncompromised bliss that she brought to herself and her lover was as refined and beautiful as velvet. I felt the most comfortable when I was Velvet Sin, allowing my mind to travel to forbidden places and satisfying my appetite for unrestricted desires.

Been thinking about this for some time
Smoking a blunt, sipping some wine
Watching you as you see me
Desiring to fuck you, telepathically

Separating my lips with your eyes
Licking the glory from my thighs
Eating the apple from my tree
Draining me dry, unapologetically

Calling my passion your angel dust
Giving my body something to trust
Pulling my panties to the side
Kissing my neck as your fingers glide

But first, let me introduce myself, Velvet Sin

Make my love jones lips grin
Look back at it, I exhale again
Spread my hips and cringe
My waterfall doesn't end

Damn!
Run that shit back again and again
Nice to meet you, Velvet Sin

I never felt ashamed of who I was as long as I kept it to myself. Behind closed doors, I could open Pandora's box in my space and live harmoniously until I rocked myself to sleep. Not everyone would think kindly of someone who does not see the ugly in sex or believes that our birth bodies should not be obscured. So, once again, I created another version of myself to make others sexually comfortable and maintain an angelic persona, Jasmine Star. Seriously! I knew it was better to play the game than to be hung high on the cross or forced to wear the scarlet letter throughout my carnal eternity.

Throughout life, folks in my space advised me to postpone sexual intercourse until I married. Subsequently, my spouse advised me to do the same. My goodness! I was married and sexually frustrated more times than I could imagine. Not that we didn't have sex, but something inside me wanted my hair pulled and my ass cuffed, which never happened. Hell, after a while, missionary did not even exist. I remember being upset with myself one day for wasting my time pretending to be sexually satisfied when I wanted and needed more. Jasmine was boring as hell, and she never experienced an orgasm.

Watch me at his door for all his neighbors to see
Coat barely covered my ass thigh highs licking on me

Door opens to my delight as his mouth says trick or treat
Heels comfortable as hell so my mouth takes a seat

Whispering slowly in my ear as his glory fills my space
Willing to be his prisoner even though I won my case

Knowing that only dark chocolate satisfies his appetite
Even though he is depleted he begs for another bite

Chapter Nine

Honest Thief

E verything I was battling, including religion, had me gasping for air in a room full of oxygen. I needed a break from the voices that were not in my head. I could not breathe and I could not sleep. When I visited the doctor for my breathing and asthma assessment, he informed me that my lungs only functioned at 68%. I mumbled why me a thousand times as he discussed medications. I asked him what would happen if the new medication did not work. He said, "Well, if the meds don't work, eventually your lungs will give out and you will die." Perfect. One more reality to add to my fight for survival.

I had no problem processing the doctor's words since I dealt with asthma for years. It sucks! Having an asthma attack is like being a fish flopping on the side of the shore because it has been out of water too long. Now that the assessment was complete, it was time to go to the doctor for something to help me sleep. Hopefully, that appointment will be on a more positive note.

As dreaded, I was diagnosed with insomnia. My first prescription was a low dose and provided no reprieve.

After some discussion, my doctor increased my dosage. Thank goodness! I was excited and eager to get some rest. Oh no. Even with the increased dosage, sleep evaded me. One night, at my wit's end, I decided to double the dosage. I accompanied the prescription with a bottle of wine and over-the-counter sleeping pills. Finally, I was able to get some rest. I slept the entire night through! It felt amazingly energizing. I had finally found the perfect concoction for sleep.

The only downfall was that to keep my body rested, I needed more prescription pills. Unfortunately, this regimen caught the attention of my doctor, who stopped refilling my medicine. I was desperate and had no choice but to start "borrowing" medication from others. After realizing what a good night's sleep felt like, I was determined to chase that feeling at any cost. Little did I know I was well on my way to addiction. I was becoming dependent on opioids. The desire to knock the edge off soon consumed not only my nights but also my days. That was my song and dance: one pill in the morning and two pills or so at night.

I vividly remember running out of my prescription pills one day and finding someone's hydrocodone in their pantry. Hydrocodone was one of my pills of choice, so I knew it would help me get through the day. My sister was taking me to a doctor's appointment, and I needed to relax. On the way there, I started having problems breathing and felt jittery inside. Even though I rolled down the window and puffed on my inhaler, I felt lightheaded. As we parked and walked towards the doctor's building, my sister asked what was wrong. I had no choice but to tell her that I had taken someone's medication, and it could not have been what I thought. We stopped in the parking lot as she tried to calm my spirit and get me to relax. We could not even reach the building's door without her repeatedly coaching me to take deep breaths. I was squeezing her hand so hard! That was scary. Lesson learned. From then on, I vowed only to use my prescribed medications.

A few months later, I was getting ready for work when my heart started beating so fast that it felt like it would jump out of my chest. I could not even form sensible sentences. I called my doctor again and asked for more medication. She had previously said no, until I came in for a checkup. State law required me to see my doctor every thirty days since my medications were considered controlled substances. I did not know what that meant, and I figured it was another way for healthcare to make more money. Anyway, my work schedule had me traveling so much that it was not easy to get in. Truthfully, I did not want to face the doctor because she knew I had refilled the medication at different pharmacies more often than I should have. I needed my prescription. I was desperate.

When she said no, I called my manager at the company I worked for and told her how sick I was. She asked me to call the company nurse. It was then that I learned that I was having withdrawals. The nurse said that if I did not get the medication, I needed to go to the hospital because I could die. The nurse then called my doctor and planned for me to see her at once. It was then that I realized I had a severe problem. The doctor told me that what I was doing would get me on a state list, where I could no longer get prescription drugs from any doctor. I broke down crying. I am unsure whether it was because I would not be able to get the medication or that I would be on a denied list for prescription drugs. It turns out that doctors typically put people on the medications I was taking for a brief period of time. When I started seeing her, I had been on them for a few years. She said she had no idea how I was still alive with the cocktail combination of clonazepam and hydrocodone. My heart should have stopped beating in my sleep. I needed help, and I needed it quickly, or else I would sleep forever.

Sometimes shit changes you, and it's not always for the best. Some trials do not elevate you, but leave you broken and a shell of the person you used to be. It shifts your identity's dynamics. When you look in the mirror, it is a stranger looking back. No more living, only existing in a stranger's body that looks and sounds like you but is someone you do not recognize. Who let you into my home, my space, my soul? Soon, you will not dress the same, you will not smile the same, and you will not survive the same.

It was time for me to face my demons instead of becoming one. I was ready to acknowledge my pain and address life's disappointments. I needed to get to know myself all over again and be honest about the destructive behavior that I labeled "healing." My first step was purging myself of lies and living in the truth of my pain. I needed to feel it, be it, own it, and let it go.

I have lost the mark and cannot see
The pain inside is overwhelming me
Reaching for strength that isn't there
Searching for hope for my soul to spare
Death is calling even in my dreams
The end is near and no peace it brings
Amid broken pieces I am beyond lost
Spent out on denial at a heaping cost
Masqueraded calm is the devil's grin
Hurt and pain are my only friends
A prisoner of heartache wanting to be free
Angels in heaven say a prayer for me

I went to my stash of random pills, took all of them out of each bottle, and counted them. I am not sure why. Maybe so I could see what I was throwing away. I remember putting all the medicines back in their bottles and thinking that getting rid of them was a bit extreme. I mean, I could control how much I took, and I would make sure I did not mix certain ones. Right? Wrong. Even though some meds had expired, I convinced myself they were still good for at least another year. Inhale. Exhale. I had to do this. I took all of the bottles, except one, to the dumpster and threw them away. I stood there for a moment. It was like I was performing a eulogy. Then I smiled. I was committed to focusing on my doctor's regimen to wing myself off all prescription pills. That meant that the last bottle had to go in the trash too. I was committed to healing my mind, body, and spirit. It was time to shed old skin and rise stronger, wiser, and more determined from the ashes.

I have the courage to stand alone
And to face what is destroying me
I have the patience to wait my turn
When it seems things just won't be

I can fly like an eagle
I can run all the way
I can look in the face of pain
I can know it will be okay
I can climb the highest mountain
I can swim to the other shore
I can feel hope rays of sunlight
I can live in abundance and more

No one has to approve my journey
Or applaud me while on the way
I don't have to dilute my pain

To find strength in life to stay

I know what it means to be still
When I don't know which way to turn
I know what it means to lean
On the lessons from life I've learned

I can fly like an eagle
I can run all the way
I can look in the face of pain
I can know it will be okay
I can climb the highest mountain
I can swim to the other shore
I can feel hope rays of sunlight
I can live in abundance and more

I can survive the treacherous storm
Regardless of where chaos may flow
Stumbling taught me how to walk
Now I shall run like never before

I believe in something bigger
That empowers me to press on
That rejuvenates my inner being
When inside all hope seems gone

I can fly like an eagle
I can run all the way

I can look in the face of pain
I can know it will be okay
I can climb the highest mountain
I can swim to the other shore
I can feel hope rays of sunlight
I can live in abundance and more

Note to Self: Fly Like an Eagle

What if I gave up as a baby? What if I decided I liked the sitting thing and did not want to do anything else? I heard I could crawl. But I also heard that it was too much work. Plus, babies were getting carpet burns, bumping into stuff, and taking forever to get somewhere. So, I decided, "I think I will just sit for the rest of my life." But then what if I decided, "I don't like this sitting all the time. I hear that if I sit long enough and wiggle with it, I can crawl. Then I heard if I crawled long enough, I could walk. And if I walked long enough, I could run!" I did it! Look at me run! Now it was time to fly. The only requirement was to fly like an Eagle.

1. **Eagles fly alone at high altitudes.** No other bird can reach the height of an eagle. Eagles have a principle: they stay away from sparrows and ravens and only fly with other Eagles.
2. **Eagles have powerful vision.** When an Eagle sets his sights on what he wants, he goes after it regardless

of the circumstances; the Eagle will always maintain his focus.

3. **When it storms, eagles get excited.** Eagles do not fear the fierce winds because the Eagle uses the wind from the storm to fly even higher. Before the Eagle knows it, he soars above the clouds and the storm.

4. **Eagles know when to rest.** When an eagle gets feeble and cannot fly as high as he once could, he finds a hiding place to rest. While there, he plucks every feather from his body and waits until new, strong feathers grow. Then, he is ready to fly again.

Chapter Ten

Beautiful Eviction

I always wondered what it would be like to meet my soul mate and feel safe with someone on cloudy days, just as much as I did when the sun was shining. Someone who never made me feel less than the beautiful treasure I was, and who endlessly cultivated the love we were blessed to share. To that person, I would give everything. Even the parts of me I hid from the world. My authentic self would finally have a majestic place to call home.

Providing support to others when they made mistakes, needed a shoulder to cry on, or when life was falling apart came natural for me. I knew how to be supportive even if no words needed to be spoken. Like those moments when someone needs you close to unpack all their heavy load and leave it where it lay. I learned how to forgive those I loved quickly, and I always believed in communicating and moving on because time was too precious to waste. However, no one has ever shown me unwavering support and love I gave to others. No one.

Love has always been subject to conditions. If I dated the right person, did the right thing, dressed a certain way, and said the correct words, the restrictions of love were never-ending. I never knew the love I had given or longed for. The one that makes me feel comfortable pulling off my mask, knowing there would be blemishes and craters of life experiences but that would be okay. At this stage in my life, I have resolved that perhaps having that type of relationship was not meant for me. Maybe it was only meant for me to share that level of love with everyone else.

I used to cry about it, pour two ounces of Angel Envy over ice, and saturate my brain about it. But one day, I put on my red slip dress, curled my hair, slid into some four-inch red pumps, and went to my private spot for an old-fashioned. It was under dimmed lights and smooth sounds from a vinyl that I decided to give myself the love I longed for. That day, I became my soul mate.

It was a journey to find sanctuary in my skin. There were no detours and very few paved roads. It took time. But after I put in all the work, life was more fulfilling. I finally appreciated the totality of who I was. Suddenly, the quiet moments did not seem so loud, and the loud moments did not seem so unbearable. My soul was moving towards unpolluted tranquility, unaffected by opinions or disapprovals. The journey of truth and honesty revealed layers of myself I didn't know existed. Even though some seemed familiar, they ran more profoundly than I ever could have imagined. Clearing my mind unleashed positivity and confidence that disrupted the bullshit in my life, and I knew I would never be the same. Finally, I could savor the taste of absolute love - my love, self-love.

I was ready to shed old habits, break mental chains of bondage, establish beliefs, and challenge ideologies. I was at a pivotal moment, and my life's purpose was to evolve mentally, physically, and spiritually. My thirst for perspicacity was desirable not only in this life but also in the hereafter. Even in the valley of death, I wanted to be satisfied. I had reached the critical crossroads where elevation was the only possibility for a meaningful life. I had reached the peak of my journey, where life demanded that I think bigger, become wiser, and metamorphose into a better version of myself.

All the years and moments spent grinning, pretending, and living other people's truth paralyzed me from discovering my own. I remember multiple times becoming celibate for months that seemed like years simply because someone said it was required for me to clear my mind. My mind was clear: I wanted to have sex! I even remember changing my hippie carefree style to equate to a person's conservative dress ensemble that they were not even following. It was evident that living a lie was not much of a life. But I did it so often until it became second nature. I believed the rhetoric about my life. My salvation, my worth, my demise, my good, my evil, my promise, and even my hope were predicated on others. I bought into it like it was my ticket to a land flowing milk and honey.

I did not realize that some people lived the exact life they said I shouldn't. The harder they criticized me, the more skeletons they had in their closet. Some of them did not even have skeletons. Heck, they had living, breathing bodies! While I lived my truth and got banished, they lived their lie and got elevated among men. It was time to sit down, grab a pen and paper, and rediscover the woman in the mirror. It was time for a beautiful eviction.

Chapter Eleven

No Compromise

The feeling of not being good enough, worrying about what others thought, and succumbing to low self-esteem evolved from not using my inner strength to protect what I valued most. Inadvertently, not setting boundaries on what I would not allow led me to allow anything and everything. People would tell me they knew me better than I knew myself, yet they knew nothing about what I was going through or the battle wounds across my heart.

Most of what I felt was self-inflicted:

- Not telling people no
- Not doing what was best for me
- Not speaking up when silence should not have been an option

My first objective was to foster the mindset of not becoming consumed with the frailties and troubles of life. Some life circumstances played with my mind, making me believe I was not as strong as I thought and could never climb the mountain before me. Going through struggles often resulted in becoming a shell of who I was, and sometimes, when I look back on those moments, it is difficult for me to recognize myself. Life can take you on journeys that strip away the essence of your soul, the breath of your being, and the solidity of your mind, so much so that you may not even realize that you are on the verge of doing things you could never undo. Setting boundaries is vital for avoiding self-hatred and self-annihilation.

While going through some of the lowest points of my life, suicide was one of the contemplated options. My brain could not handle the mental chaos occurring 24/7. At the same time, I despised myself for being weak. I was so petrified of being "weak" that I would not ask for help. Instead, I found myself in oblivion quicksand. At the same time, I was resisting the urge to seek help while simultaneously yearning for it. I became a recluse. All I wanted to do was stay in the house and shun the world.

One day, I went online and typed the word suicide in a Google search. When I hit ENTER, all these websites popped up. I randomly picked one, and it turned out to be a blog that started with, "Before you decide which way to commit suicide, first do these things." I was curious, so I continued reading.

Do you have people who would miss you? It could be your family, friends, co-workers, or anyone else who would think about you if you were gone. I thought, yes. *Since suicide is selfish, the least* you can do is the unselfish act of making things easier for those who love and will miss you. When you are gone, they will be too distraught to think. Here is a list of things to do before suicide.

1) *List the names of all the people who would miss you.* I got a piece of paper and started listing names. I decided to write family first. I was still listing names after two hours. My hand was hurting so much that I had to take a break. But I kept reading.

2) *State how your absence would make each name feel.* Once again, I returned to listing names and fell asleep. The task was excruciating. After my nap, I went back to reading. *When you get done, if you still want to commit suicide, go to the next step.* I remember thinking, this is a lot of work. I have not even finished number one. It will take days and weeks to complete the first steps. I kept reading.

3) *Make a list of all your personal information including your bank account numbers, passwords, how much money you have in each account, your current & previous mailing addresses, your social security number, and your passport.* The list continued with about fifty to sixty things. *If you still want to commit suicide, continue on.*

4) *Pack everything in your place with detailed labels, put it in storage, and pay your storage up for a year to give time for your loved ones to grieve. If you still want to commit suicide, then...*

Finally, I realized that this article was not about how to commit suicide but about the impact of suicide on those you love and on those who love you. I was overwhelmed reading the list of things to do and was exhausted when I got to the end and read, *If you made it to the end of reading this, you should not want to take your life. The fact that you read to the end shows you care, someone cares for you, and you are worth fighting for.*

I was lucky to have found that blog. It made me think about the aftermath of taking my own life. There are many stories where people were on the verge of letting go, but someone grabbed their hand and gave them the strength to hold on and the encouragement to fight. For me, my angel was a Google blog.

I read an article about a young man who was about to jump and end his life on a bridge. While he was there, a man drove by, stopped, and ran to him. The man inquired if he needed assistance and what he was doing on the bridge. With tears rolling down his face and defeat in his voice, the young man started naming everything wrong in his life and how he had no reason to live. The stranger extended his hand and said, "If you don't jump, I promise you your life will get better, and I will make sure of it." Because a random stranger showed love, this young man got the help he needed. Years later, he married, had children, and is enjoying a wonderful life.

Instead of concentrating on ending my life, I began a new one. I started making plans for what I wanted my life to look like. In this new life, none of my happiness, joy, self-confidence, or peace would be at the mercy of anyone again. That mindset brought my inner strength out of the rubble of life that always existed inside. It was time to set boundaries and be honest. When someone did something that made me feel uncomfortable or had an energy that did not align with mine, I had to be honest. That did not mean I would address negative vibes every time something happened. It meant I would be self-aware, reflect on the situation, and weigh if it even called for me to take it personally. My focus shifted to being conscious of people's behavior and attitudes towards me, balanced with not letting their egocentrics impact my peace or how I move. I can choose which battles are worth fighting and which to avoid. It is a great feeling. I no longer care if people think I have an attitude problem or am funny. Sometimes, it is necessary to have an attitude problem. Other times, I have found peace in silence, allowing things to be.

Years ago, someone close to me shared that what I said did not go over well and made him feel bad. That broke my heart. The first thing I did was thank him for sharing how he felt, and the second thing I did was look inward and vow not to portray that behavior again. A relationship is not valuable if someone cannot come to you when you hurt them and vice versa.

Someone once said, "People or situations cannot hurt you. You can determine if you will be happy, sad, or hurt." To that person, I politely respond, "Bullshit!" If words, attitudes, demeaning behavior, or ridicule could be eliminated by me simply saying, "It did not hurt, and I am happy," I am pretty sure there would be no need for counselors, psychologists, confessions, silent retreats, meditations, or all of the other options that help one be centered again and learn how to deal with bullshit.

I am just as passionate about acknowledging hurt as I am about keeping the promise I made to own my feelings. I only have the power to change myself. If someone does not care about my mental well-being or is offensive, I will oblige and choose not to be around them. I do not need to discuss it. Boundaries are necessary. I will not worry about or try to change someone. I will not expect certain people to care about me feeling comfortable in their space. Perhaps their space is not the best place for me. Actual growth is when you reach a level of wisdom without needing to prove anything. That is where true happiness lies for me.

I promised to identify what makes me happy and cultivate a life of happiness. Growing up, whenever I wanted to put a smile on my face or forget the day's worries, I would lay on the concrete hill of my childhood home driveway or in the back of my dad's truck, looking at the moonlight and stars. I remember looking at the moon and saying, "Hello, my friend. I see you are shining bright tonight." I am glad no one heard me because they would have thought I was crazy! But under the moonlight, I felt like the whole universe was smiling at me. I was safe from getting caught up in living the narrative other people had for me, which resulted in me losing myself little by little.

Little things, like wearing my skirts down to my ankles instead of how I liked them, above my knees; listening to music they preferred instead of my country tunes; and trying to be calm, quiet, and reserved so people would not think I was too hyper or had too much energy. All that made me miss being my fabulous, bohemian, quirky self with blonde roots. After all those years and moments, I realized that I only succeeded in suppressing my true self. So now, I embrace my uniqueness and refuse to compromise it for anyone.

The last boundary I set for myself was to be intentional about how I love and treat myself. This mindset allowed me to swim through raging waters when I did not know how to swim. It allowed me to navigate rough terrain without a compass, insight, or directions. There is something magical about embracing who you are, loving who you are, and accepting who you are. I will forgive myself, frequently cleanse my spirit of negativity, and appreciate who I am. There is something invigorating about honesty. If it hurts, it hurts. If it's good, it's good. And I promise that life will be great, with no regrets and no compromise.

Chapter Twelve

Inner Peace

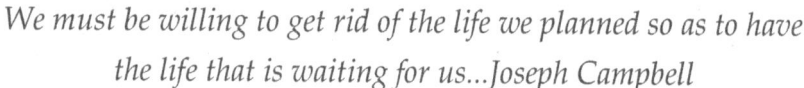

We must be willing to get rid of the life we planned so as to have the life that is waiting for us...Joseph Campbell

I have finally reached a place where I feel mentally, spiritually, and emotionally safe, where walls do not exist, and there is no need to draw lines in the sand for battle. For most of my life, I was afraid that people would see the real me and be disappointed. The real me is vulnerable, needs hugs and kisses, appreciates affirmations, and desires pure acceptance. I never felt secure enough to be imperfect, so I hid my true self for years, even to my detriment. But today is a new day. It is time for me to focus on myself without being apologetic. Call me selfish, inconsiderate, or self-absorbed; I will be all that and more from this moment forward.

I find reminiscing to be healthy for my soul. However, I do not dwell on the past. I realize that the mistakes I made in the past were opportunities to learn and grow. Sometimes, it took me years of not learning a lesson, but when it finally happened, it was clear. One valuable lesson I learned was that there will always be people who find fault with you, regardless of your sex, sexuality, faith, religion, money, or lifestyle. I have tried to prove this theory wrong, but it has always held. For example, even if I went to church all the time, people would still ridicule me for being tardy just once. If I wore dresses that swept the floor 364 days of the year and on day 365 wore a dress above my ankles, someone would say I was being fresh. If I gave up meat but had to get me some Popeyes spicy fried chicken one day, people would say I was a fraudster. Eventually, I realized that fault-finding was human nature. So, I decided to do what makes me happy, regardless of what others think. The fact is that no matter what you do, someone is waiting in the bushes to scream, SHAME, SHAME, SHAME! When I started focusing on my truth, my life became more rewarding. However, that does not mean that my life was perfect. All of my stories don't have happy endings, and not all of my truths are warm and fuzzy. Some realities are not pretty.

I realized that there were things about myself that I did not like. I despised certain aspects of myself. It was easy to get caught in the notion that "that's just the way you are" and that I would always be that way. However, I recognized that this did not define my ability to grow, expand my horizons, and become a better person. Once I acknowledged the negative aspects of myself, it was up to me to act. One day, I decided to have a frank discussion with me, myself, and I. "Why don't you change the things you don't like?" I realized how powerful I was when I accepted that the things I disliked about myself were due to my refusal to change. So, I made a list of things that did not add value to my life and worked on chipping away at them every day. I took ownership of my failures and mistakes without blaming anyone else. I focused on my contribution to the chaos, as that was the only part of the scenario I could change. Doing so made me determined to control what I could and let the rest be.

In the past, I spent a lot of energy analyzing things and people beyond my control. However, I could have used that energy to focus on figuring out my course of action and enjoying life. When I focused on what I could do to improve myself, I started valuing myself more and gained greater self-worth and self-esteem. This newfound self-worth became the foundation of how I viewed others and how they perceived me. It was time for me to begin living in my power. Instead of seeing myself as I was, I began to see myself as I could be. I incorporated principles into my life that helped me release my inner strength.

Dream

There is power in dreams. Dreams are known to uplift, give hope, and provide a gateway for a brighter and more powerful existence. Before drifting off to sleep, I listen to motivational speeches, meditation ensembles, or positive affirmations. I have the power to condition my mind even while I sleep.

Step Outside

A motivational speaker once said, "What if stepping into the unknown is stepping into fulfilling your dreams and desires? But, because of fear, you never see your dreams come to fruition." I had to change my thought process to believe that being outside my comfort zone was my comfort zone. So, I began challenging ideas, raising my hand, and embracing the opportunities within the unknown.

Let Go

Finding the ability to give myself the freedom not to be perfect was my first step to letting go. Focusing on past disappointments and regrets from yesterday was like driving a car without ever replacing flat tires. Soon, there is little to no momentum. Letting go empowered me to release myself from my past and inspired me to walk into a brighter tomorrow.

Have Joy

The beauty of joy is that it comes from within and permeates one's existence. Joy is a more profound experience than happiness. Happiness exists because of something, but joy exists regardless of something. Here's another way to think about it. Homeowner insurance protects my home in uncontrollable and unanticipated circumstances. Without it, my house is left at the mercy of chance. Even amid the destruction, when I have joy, I can rest assured that I will remain whole.

Be a Warrior

David Goggins is someone who redefines everything he touches and inspires millions. He overcame abuse, depression, poverty, and sickle cell anemia to serve in the Air Force as a Navy Seal, becoming one of the most remarkable endurance athletes in the world. David Goggins: Be a Warrior, "Heraclitus, a philosopher born in the Persian Empire back in the fifth century BC, had it right when he wrote about men on the battlefield. Out of every one-hundred men," he wrote, "ten shouldn't even be there, eighty are just targets, nine are the real fighters, and we are lucky to have them, for they make the battle. Ah, but the one, one is a warrior... Be the 1% of people willing to do what it takes. Be the warrior. The warrior trains, battles, and never backs down." To achieve the unattainable, being a warrior is the only way.

Don't Make Lemonade

There is a cliché' that says, "When given lemons, make lemonade." I admonish myself to give the lemons back instead. I practice this behavior when a friend or family decides to enlighten me with their negative perspectives; I look, listen, and at the end, I smile and say, "I see," and walk away. If they send text laced with crap, I read it, and instead of trying to figure out the perfect rebuttal, I do not respond. I realize that I do not have to respond to negativity. When I accept everything a person or situation throws at me, I am at the mercy of circumstance. I am taking control of my thoughts and perspectives.

****

People often say sustainable resources are saving the earth; being sustainable means maintainable and sound. It also means resources are valued as scarce, understanding that if not guarded or used wisely, one day they will no longer be accessible. My thoughts, behavior, beliefs, energy, and soul should be regarded as rare and appreciated. For years, I treated myself like I could return to the source and draw from my reserve when depleted. But what if one day I went to draw and nothing was there? Or I needed something rare and beautiful but no clue where to find it? Life brought me so often to an impasse that something had to change. Before I became extinct, I had to start purging myself of the people, the past, and the thoughts that made me feel unloved, unwanted, and unvalued.

Finding my way required me to relearn concepts that were embedded in my core. It was time to change the narrative. For me, power used to mean not showing emotions, not being vulnerable, and hiding who I was. It protected everyone else's happiness, even if it meant sacrificing mine. Now, power means sharing who I am, being open to being open, and finding calm while being weak. Surprisingly, every time I walked with my new power, I became stronger. I was able to walk around with my walls down. I was able to smile when people opposed me. I was able to remain silent when I disagreed with narratives. It was like having a newfound peace. I was even able to welcome love in friendships and relationships. I was no longer worried about if someone would hurt me or lie to me. My energy was spent being present and embracing the moment. I finally knew what it felt like to have power that no one could take away.

When my inner being told me to move, I knew it was time for me to take the road less traveled. Every step gave me the strength I needed for the journey. How often have I heard that life is a personal journey? Yet everyone felt that they had my roadmap. I started trusting in my path, trusting in my direction, and trusting in my walk. So, when people became skeptical and critical about my approach, I could boldly say, "My path was not intended for you. Therefore, our levels of understanding should not align. If my path leads me closer to inner peace, then that is the road I will travel, even if I must travel alone."

Things others would not accept
They thought I'd understand
I was always saying YES
So my weakness was the plan

They saw me walking in pain
Heard my ache in every stride
But it was easier to turn away
While my heart decayed inside

Always been the chosen one
The willing sacrificial lamb
Whenever they needed me
Wait a minute here I am

Same time they say thank you
I'm called a fool behind my back
Wanting to please the masses
Took my focus out of whack

If it took this to go to heaven
Then usher me straight to hell
Mistreated and misused for life
A combination no longer for sale

Kiss my ass kiss my ass
To those who mistreated me
Look at that no fucks to give
The sacrificial lamb is now free

Chapter Thirteen

The Resurrection

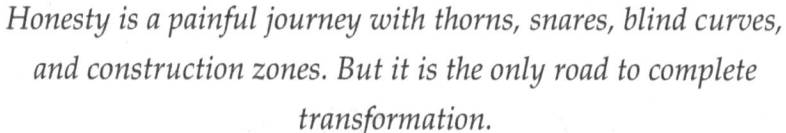

Honesty is a painful journey with thorns, snares, blind curves, and construction zones. But it is the only road to complete transformation.

One of my favorite things is going to the beach at sunrise and having mimosas. Feeling the sand between my toes and watching the moonlight simultaneously dance with the sun's warm colors is enchanting. I admire how the sun's rising and the moon's coming down shimmer brilliantly as one on the water waves. The beauty is captivating. Sometimes, I close my eyes and go there while sitting at home. I can hear the crashing waves and the silence around me. No one is there except me. As I run my fingers through the sand, my body becomes one with the earth. I am at peace. The best music at the moment is nothing at all. My mimosa is ninety percent champagne with a cranberry and orange juice splash. Now, my drink resembles what I see. I place the champagne bottle down and begin to walk on the shore. It feels like the world belongs to me. As far as I can see, there is peace. It is there I sit and begin to write.

A Letter to Me

A Letter to Me From Me

Remember before you were born into this world? Of course, you don't! But it happened, and I am sure the world was full of glee to have you join this journey. I want to warn you that no magical spell or elaborate book can guarantee you a smooth ride. You will be hurt, break a few bones, stump your toe, and get a few splinters. You will think and say one thing, but people may perceive it differently. You will cry, become frustrated, and sometimes feel alone. But even with all that rigor, life will still be worthwhile.

Do not get discouraged when the glass is half empty instead of half full. Keep going even when everything you touch seems to fail. And do not give into the snares of rejection and ridicule. You will feel heartache, isolation, and like giving up. But do not. If you hold on, you will realize that everything you overcome fortifies you into BEAUTY & BEAST.

The beauty in you will resonate with kindness and understanding. You will be sensitive to those in need and a beacon of hope to those in despair. Your words will touch hearts and inspire people who have gone through some of the same quicksand that almost claimed their lives. Through you, they will know that life goes on and that they are worth the fight. When you encourage others to walk in their path, you will embrace where they are in life, and without judgment support where they are going. You will make friends with people from various social classes and begin to appreciate diversity with love. The best beauty resonates from within, and even through blemishes, it appears incredible. This will be your beauty and strength. So do not hide from your anguish. It is the foundation of your power. Embrace the ups and downs, because you will need both to appreciate growth and success. One day, on the other side, you will wake up to a new you, a better you, a more brilliant you, and a wiser you. And when you do that, you can share true beauty with the world.

That is just a fraction of what you will share with the world, for you are not only Beauty but also Beast. You are resilient. You will work to become a reckoning force that sometimes you will not even recognize. You will be able to stare enemies, tribulations, uncertainty, and bitterness in the face and smile because you will be equipped with the mental ability to survive and conquer. Life will take you on many rollercoasters, so you will not be afraid of the next uncertain ride. You will be mindful of your capability and no longer intimidated by the thorns of life. When you feel tired, you will be able to rest and recharge.

You will never give up. You'll understand that your goals may change, but the essence of achieving them will not. Trying again and again will become second nature and part of your DNA. It is in the trying that you will find success. More time will be spent alone accomplishing personal goals and learning what motivates you. Your endurance will stay in beast mode. While others may think beast means cruel, monster, or barbaric, you will show that it means determined, unwavering, and fierce. This is what it will take for you to rise. And rise you shall.

Stay focused on what is important to you. Never compromise your integrity for superficial gratification. Protect your peace. It is within your peace that you will find clarity. Get prepared, be prepared, and always stay prepared. Always remember who you are and what you have to offer and share that beauty unapologetically with the world. And when necessary, never hesitate to let the world know that this Beauty is also Beast.

I am proud of how you inspire
And I am happy to call you my own
When I think of the hills you climbed
And the fears you have faced alone
I see strength and I see hope
Even when drenched in pain
I see life during despair
Even when your soul is drained
It is remarkable the lessons of life
They get easier as time goes on
If you keep going and don't faint
I promise you will be strong
You will shake ashes of depression
Your sight will encourage the blind
You will hold your head up proudly
Regardless of mistakes behind
This life has limited guarantees
But this one thing I know is true
Your Beauty and Your Beast await
The Resurrection was waiting for you

Resources

SUICIDE

Do you know how many people have thought about suicide, attempted suicide, or know someone who has taken their life? According to the CDC:

12 million people – contemplated suicide

3.5 million people – made plans for suicide

1.7 million people – attempted suicide

In the last twenty years, the suicide rate has increased by nearly 40%.

If you or someone you know needs support, please call 988. For those in the United States, this confidential 24/7 free lifeline is available in English and Spanish. You can also chat online by going to https://988lifeline.org. Support is also available for the blind, veterans, and those with loss of hearing.

Source:
Suicide Data and Statistics | Suicide Prevention | CDC
https://www.cdc.gov/suicide/facts/data.html

MENTAL HEALTH

More than ever, we are facing life perils that challenge our resilience and can change our ability to function at our best. Mental health is the foundation of our health; it determines how we heal and can decrease our quality of life. Every individual faces these challenges, and no one is immune to them.

Facts from National Alliance on Mental Illness (NAMI):

- 46% of people who die by suicide had a diagnosed mental health condition
- Across the U.S. economy, serious mental illness causes $193.2 billion in lost earnings each year
- Depression and anxiety disorders cost the global economy $1 trillion in lost productivity each year

If you or someone you know needs support the NAMI Help Line is available 10 a.m. – 10 p.m. ET weekdays. Call 800-950-6264, text "helpline" to 62640, or chat online. In a crisis, call or text 988 (24/7). You can also find information for your local NAMI by going to https://www.nami.org/About-Mental-Illness.

Source:
Mental Health by the Numbers | NAMI
https://www.nami.org/About-Mental-Illness/Mental-Health-By-the-Numbers